Introduction

A lot of *Blade* is true. It happened to me as a
schoolboy when I was the victim of a bully just like
Toxon. This play is based on the story I wrote
about it many years later.

Mind you, it can be tricky to make a play out of
a story – even a true story. With a story you only
need one voice because you tell it. With a play you
need several voices because you show it. Luckily, I'd
put a lot of talk into the story-version of *Blade*. So
it wasn't hard to transfer this talk into the
play-version. After that, I linked the different
scenes with a Narrator (a sort of story-telling
voice).

By the time I'd finished I couldn't decide which I
liked better – the story of *Blade* or the play of *Blade*!
Maybe you should read both and make up your own
mind …

For Jake, Polly and Suzie ...
when they're old enough

Blade

by

Chris Powling

Based on the gr8read novel *Blade*
by Chris Powling

First published in 2009 in Great Britain by
Barrington Stoke Ltd
18 Walker St, Edinburgh, EH3 7LP

www.barringtonstoke.co.uk

Copyright © 2009 Chris Powling

The moral right of the author has been asserted in
accordance with the Copyright, Designs and
Patents Act 1988

ISBN: 978-1-84299-642-3

Printed in Great Britain by Bell & Bain Ltd

Contents

Cast

Narrator

The narrator fills in parts of the story.

Stage Manager

The stage manager tells us where and when it is all taking place.

Rich

Rich, the hero, is a new boy. He meets the school bully in a dark passage, where there is nobody who can help him.

Lee

Lee is Rich's rather mad friend who has only one eye.

Toxon

Toxon is the school bully.

Minder 1

Minder 1 is one of Toxon's mates.

Minder 2

Minder 2 is also one of Toxon's mates.

Big Kid

The Big Kid scares the new boys by telling them to keep away from Toxon or else ...

Introduction

Narrator: This play is set more than fifty years ago. Some of it really happened. Toxon was the sort of bully no one spoke about in those days. Today, most of his victims would tell a teacher at once and get the help they needed. Maybe Toxon would get the help *he* needed, too.

Scene 1

The Playground at Upper School

Stage Manager: The first day of term at Upper School. The playground is full of new kids.

Rich: You look smart, Lee!

Lee: You too, Rich. New blazer, new shoes, new school bag …

Rich: You've even got a new eye-patch.

Lee: Mum made it for me. She said I'd scare all the other kids if I didn't wear it. What do you think, Rich? I was born with this bad eye. Does it still look like a peeled grape?

Rich: Well ...

Lee: OK, no need to be polite. Remember how I used to terrify the little kids at our last school? They ran off yelling every time I lifted my patch!

Rich:	You were mad in those days, Lee. But we're at Upper School now. There aren't any little kids here.
Lee:	Only us, Rich.
Rich:	Yeah ... only us.
Big Kid:	Hey ... are you two new kids?
Rich:	Yes, we are.
Big Kid:	Then let me tell you something ... something very important. Stay away from Toxon!

Rich:	Toxon?
Lee:	Who's Toxon?
Big Kid:	You mean you don't know who Toxon is?
Rich:	Never heard of him.
Big Kid:	Then you'd better find out fast ... before Toxon finds out about you.

Scene 2

A Corner of the Playground

Stage Manager: A corner of the playground at lunch time. It's still the first day of term.

Narrator: By now, all the new kids had heard of Toxon. His name was on everyone's lips. Maybe that's why they looked so shell-shocked.

Rich: At least we haven't met him face-to-face yet.

Lee: Don't want to, either.

Rich: Nor do I, Lee. Have you heard about these party games he plays with new kids?

Lee: Yeah, I have. What about this "Blade" thing he carries? Tell me about that.

Rich: It's a knife.

Lee: A knife?

Rich: That's what the other kids are saying. But don't ask me what kind of knife.

Lee: Even the sound of it is scary ... *Blade.*

Rich: That big kid who warned us was right, Lee. Let's keep out of Toxon's way.

Lee: You bet, Rich.

Narrator: At first this seemed easy. There were 1000 other kids at Upper School, after all. Why should Toxon pick on them? Then Rich made a big mistake.

Scene 3

Behind the Gym

Stage Manager: A narrow passage behind the gym. There are big, spiky thorn bushes here and there. Apart from these the passage is empty. Or so it seems when Rich arrives.

Rich: I know this passage is out of bounds. But it's a short-cut to the Science Lab and I'm already late for the lesson. So, fingers crossed. Go for it, Rich.

Toxon: Hey, new kid ...

Rich: What?

Toxon: Come here, new kid ...

Rich: Who's that?

Toxon: I'm the worst thing that
              could happen to you, new
              kid. And I'm here behind
              this thorn bush.

Rich: Toxon?

Toxon: The very same, new kid. And
              this happens to be *my* place,
              OK?

Minder 1:	It's *your* place, Tox.
Minder 2:	That's right, Tox. It's *your* place.
Toxon:	No one comes to *my* place unless I invite them. And I haven't invited you, new kid. So what are you doing here, may I ask?
Rich:	I didn't know it was your place, Toxon. Honest, I didn't. Shall I go right now?
Toxon:	"Go right now?" I'm afraid it's not as simple as that, new kid ...

Minder 1:	No, it's not as simple as that.
Minder 2:	It's not nearly as simple as that ...
Toxon:	You see, there's the matter of payment.
Rich:	Payment?
Toxon:	Payment, yes. For coming here when you haven't been invited.
Rich:	But I haven't got any money.
Toxon:	No money?
Minder 1:	No money?

Minder 2:   No money?

Toxon: Dear me. No money, eh? In that case, new kid, let's have your hymn book.

Rich: My hymn book?

Toxon: It's in the top pocket of your blazer. With your name inside it. That's a school rule, new kid. So the masters can find out who you are.

Rich: Here it is.

Toxon: Thanks, new kid. I'm glad you're sticking to the school rules. Now ... are you ready?

Rich: Ready?

Toxon: For a party game.

Minder 1: Yeah, a party game.

Minder 2: Just a party game, that's all.

Narrator: Rich gave a shudder. He'd been expecting this. But why the hymn book? And why were Toxon's minders looking so jumpy? Had they played this game before?

Scene 4

Still Behind the Gym

Stage Manager: Still in the passage behind the gym. The day seems to have got darker. The rest of Upper School has never felt so far away.

Toxon: You a good reader, new kid?

Rich: Pretty good, yes.

Toxon: Can you read a hymn for me ... without making any mistakes?

Rich: I think so.

Toxon: Good. Because that's what
                 you've got to do in this party
                 game of mine. It goes like
                 this. I choose a hymn and
                 you read it out loud.
                 Without making a single
                 mistake. Are you with me so
                 far?

Rich: What if I do make a mistake?

Toxon: Good question.

Minder 1:   Good question.

Minder 2:   Good question.

Toxon:	I'm glad you asked me that, new kid. You'll like the next bit. You see, for every mistake you make, you get a kiss.
Rich:	A kiss?
Toxon:	A kiss from my little friend.
Rich:	A kiss from your little friend? Who's that?
Toxon:	That's another good question.
Minder 1:	Another good question, Tox.

Minder 2:	Yeah, it's another good question.
Toxon:	Would you like to meet my little friend?
Rich:	Right now, you mean?
Toxon:	I mean very much right now.
Narrator:	Toxon slid a hand in his blazer pocket. When he took it out again he was holding the handle of a knife. Just the handle, that's all – a handle about as long as a pencil.

Toxon: This is my little friend, new kid. And here's how she gives you a kiss ...

Scene 5

Darkness

Stage Manager: A black cloud has covered the sky. It's so dark behind the thorn bush that Rich can hardly see the three bullies.

Toxon: Are you ready, new kid?

Rich: Ready.

Toxon: So am I.

Narrator: And Toxon pressed the knife handle. At once, something flicked out that was thin and sharp. It glinted. The knife was as long as two pencils now.

Toxon: What do you think of my little friend, new kid? I call her "Blade".

Rich: Blade ...

Minder 1: Blade ...

Minder 2: Blade ...

Toxon: You know what, new kid? I think Blade has taken a real fancy to you. I can see she's longing to give you a kiss.

So let me flick her back into the knife-handle. And let me hold it level with your eye.

Rich: Level with my eye?

Toxon: You've got it! Now comes the hymn, new kid. See? I've chosen one for you already. All you've got to do is read it. Without making a single mistake. Because if you do …

Minder 1: If you do …

Minder 2: If you do, new kid …

Toxon: ... you'll get a kiss, OK? A teeny-tiny little kiss from my teeny-tiny little friend who lives right here in the knife-handle. One kiss for every mistake. One kiss flicked at your eye-ball.

Rich *(choking):* At my ...

Toxon: ... *eye-ball.*

Narrator: Rich did his best to keep calm. He knew he mustn't panic. After all, he only had to read a hymn. What was so hard about that?

Toxon: Oh, yes. Just one other thing, new kid. Let's make the reading a bit more fun. Let's turn your hymn book upside down.

Rich: Upside down?

Narrator: Toxon flipped the hymn book over. The words on the page looked different now – as different as English is from Arabic.

Toxon: Go ahead, new kid. Read it *now*.

Scene 6

Lee's Bedroom

Stage Manager: Lee's bedroom that afternoon. Lee and Rich are just back from school. Outside, it has started to rain.

Lee: Upside down, Rich? Toxon made you read the hymn upside down?

Rich: Every word.

Lee: With the knife-blade level with your eye-ball? And his two minders just standing there, watching? You must have been scared witless!

Rich: I was scared out of my mind, Lee. I was almost messing my pants. But I was still able to read the hymn upside down.

Lee: How?

Rich: I got lucky, that's all. Toxon had chosen a hymn I knew off by heart. We used to sing it at our last school. I didn't need the hymn book at all. I just let Toxon *think* I was reading it.

Lee: So you didn't make any mistakes ...

Rich: Not one. Not even seeing Blade in the corner of my eye ready to kiss me at any moment.

Lee: He's sick, Rich. This Toxon guy is sick. He wants the whole school to be scared of him.

Rich: It already is.

Lee: Well, he's got to be stopped. If he isn't, we'll have another Hitler on our hands one day.

Rich: Or another Stalin.

Lee: Anyway, I bet he's bluffing.

Rich: Bluffing?

Lee: Toxon is all talk. Most bullies are like that. He'd crumble if you stood up to him.

Rich: Oh, yeah? Suppose he isn't like most bullies? Suppose he isn't the kind that crumbles?

Lee: Someone's got to find out, Rich. Someone's got to take that risk.

Rich: Like who?

Narrator: Lee was staring into space. His face was still white with anger. He was in one of his mad moods. Rich hadn't seen this since primary school.

Lee: Maybe someone like *me*.

Scene 7

Behind the Gym Again

Stage Manager: Toxon and his two minders are still hiding out in the thorn bushes. It's lunch time again. The passage behind the gym is as bleak and lonely as ever.

Toxon: Well, stack me! If it isn't a pair of new kids come to my place. I've met one of them before ... but not the one with the eye-patch.

Lee:	Which of these guys is Toxon, Rich?
Rich:	Him.
Lee:	You mean the small one?
Toxon:	Ho-ho-ho. I like new kids who can make a joke. So does my little friend. She sorts them out with a kiss, you know. She sorts them out real quick.
Lee:	Really? What little friend is this?
Toxon:	Here in my hand, new kid.

Lee: Oh, *that* little friend. I've heard about her. You flick her in kids' faces because you think it's scary.

Toxon: Don't you think it's scary, new kid?

Lee: Not much.

Narrator: Lee lifted a hand level with his eye-patch. He pressed a button on a pretend knife-handle. Flick! Flick! Flick!

Lee: Now that's what I call scary ... when you poke a blade in your own face.

Toxon: In your *own* face?

Lee: You hold the handle as near to your eye as you dare, Tox. Then – *flick!* – you open out the blade. That's a game that takes real guts. Not like reading a soppy hymn.

Toxon: You think so?

Lee: Hey, why don't we try it? You against me. We each take a turn with your little friend, OK? The winner is the one who gets the tip closest to his own eye-ball. Cool, eh? What do you think, Tox?

Toxon: I think it's a con, new kid. You've got con-man written all over you. You'd never take that kind of risk.

Lee: I've done it before.

Toxon: You've played this game before?

Lee: Look, I'll show you.

Narrator: Coolly, Lee shifted his eye-patch. His bad eye still looked like a peeled grape.

Toxon: You did that to yourself?

Lee: Well, you're bound to get it wrong a few times, Tox. At least to begin with. Shall we start, then? I'll have first go if you like.

Toxon: You're a nutter! What kind of a kid even thinks of a game like that?

Minder 1: Hold on, Tox. What if he is a nutter? He's still come to

our place, right? And he's
still only a new kid. Are you
taking him on or not?

Minder 2:   Make up your mind, Tox.

Toxon: But that's stupid! One slip
with Blade and I'll end up ...
I'll end up ...

Minder 1:   With an eye like his?

Lee: Ready when you are, Tox.

Toxon: No way, new kid. I've got
better things to do than
mess around with some
nutter who's only been in

the school five minutes.

Coming, you guys?

Minder 2: Not yet, Tox.

Minder 1: If ever, Tox.

Toxon: What?

Minder 2: Tox, you backed down.

Minder 1: So it's over, OK?

Toxon: Over?

Minder 1: What are you waiting for,
Tox?

Minder 2: A kiss, maybe?

Narrator:	Toxon crept away without another word. No one bothered to watch him go. Rich and the others were too busy staring at Lee and his eye-patch.
Minder 1:	Nice one, nutter.
Minder 2:	Yeah ... nice one, nutter.

Scene 8

Back in Lee's Bedroom

Stage Manager: Lee's bedroom the next day.

Lee: We did it, Rich!

Rich: *You* did it, you mean.

Lee: Who cares as long as we got rid of Toxon?

Rich: And as long as he took Blade with him.

Lee: No, he didn't. I found it under the thorn bush this morning. He must have

dropped it as he left. I broke
it into bits and dumped them
in a bin.

Rich: Trust you to finish the job,
Lee!

Narrator: And trust Lee not to show off
about it. A real hero is like
that. Remember, this
happened more than 50
years ago. Many of today's
schools have got bullies
sorted. And it's a good thing
they have. After all, Rich
was about as lucky as you
can get. We can't all be best

friends with a mad kid who

wears an eye-patch.

Thing: The Play
by
Chris Powling

Black button eyes.
Ziz-zag mouth.
Stiff body.
Thing.

Once it was Robbie's
best friend. Now it's
become his enemy ...

Mind-Set: The Play
by
Joanna Kenrick

Mark and Shaleem are
best mates.
But the bombs change
everything.
Will Mark stand up for
Shaleem when it
matters?

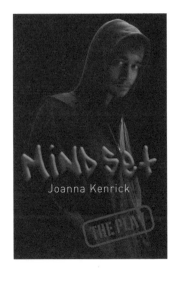

You can order these books directly from our website at
www.barringtonstoke.co.uk

**Perfect: The Play
by
Joanna Kenrick**

Too good to be true?
Dan and Kate are
perfect together.
Nothing can go wrong.
Until the lying starts.

**Alligator: The Play
by
Theresa Breslin and
Julie Gormley**

Jono has a problem.
He's just got himself an
alligator. His mum is
going to kill him. Unless
the alligator gets there
first.

You can order these books directly from our website at
www.barringtonstoke.co.uk